Ne~~x~~ton's Laws of ~~~~Motion
(PRO above, inserted before Motion)

The quintessential marketing guide to help any small business or nonprofit put promotion in motion

Written and illustrated by Leslie A.M. Smith.

Published by McCormick L.A.

Copyright © 2020 Leslie A. M. Smith All rights reserved.

No part of this book may be reproduced, or stored in a retrieval system, or transmitted in any form or by any means, electronic, mechanical, photocopying, recording, or otherwise, without express written permission of the publisher.

Cover design by Leslie A.M. Smith.

Table of Contents

TABLE OF CONTENTS III
PREFACE 1
NEWTON'S LAWS 2
BUILDING BLOCKS 7
(MARKETING MIX) 7
THE FIRST LAW 12
   How To Coordinate a Grand Opening or Open House 16
   Activity: Self-Assessment 18
   Case Study – Pint One 19
   Activity: Tactics 21
THE SECOND LAW 22
   Something to Think About – Forcing the Issue 27
   Case Study – Pint Two 29
   Pro-Tips 33
   Activity: Objectives 33
THE THIRD LAW 34
   Case Study – Pint 3 38
EVALUATION 40
   Message Assessment Tool 41
CONCLUSION 42
   Promotion Glossary 43
   Acknowledgements 45
   About the Author 46

Preface

You might not have much or any experience in marketing. You might feel like you should know more as a business owner or because you have been unceremoniously labeled the marketing director of your nonprofit.

The truth is you are not alone.

Marketing mania is a problem!

The acronyms and terms are confusing. The amount of data you can find on the Internet is overwhelming. Finally, you are afraid you don't have enough money in the budget to do much.

This guide provides the advice you need. It is all presented in no-nonsense, simple terms that anyone new to marketing and promotions can understand.

After reading this simple guide, you will master the three simple laws of promotion and feel ready to take charge and truly put it in motion.

Leslie A.M. Smith

Newton's Laws

Do you remember learning about gravity when you were in elementary school? You'll likely recall a drawing of Sir Isaac Newton with an apple falling from a tree and you learned that Earth's gravitational force keeps things falling down. So simple you learned about it when you were a child.

Discovering this force as a constant, Newton built on Johann Kepler's Laws of Planetary Motion to create what's known as Newton's Three

Laws of Promotion

Laws of Motion. Fast forward a few hundred years and we can recognize that these laws also apply to promoting a business. Eureka! What a find!

The three basic rules to follow are outlined in this guide. That's all! Don't overthink it, don't make it more complicated. Follow these three principles to start and keep your promotional activities moving in the right direction.

The bottom line is, hanging a sign is not enough. The "build it and they will come" mentality only works if the act of building is generating "buzz," meaning it is the topic of conversation around town and the media has found it interesting as well. It has to be eye-catching and different, like Walt Disney constructing Disneyland from what had been an orange grove, or more recently the Carvana car dealership building a car vending machine adjacent to the freeway.

On the contrary, it's likely your office resembles a box and won't pique much interest for the general passerby so you have to go about it another way.

Businesses (nonprofit organizations and for-profit businesses alike) need two things: customers and revenue.

If a sign alone works—and maybe it does for you, then you are in an extremely fortunate position to be filling a need that no one else is. For instance, think about the first person to sell toilet paper. A sign in a well-traveled area might be all that was needed to make that product's sales increase. At first, anyway. But what happened when another person started selling toilet paper? Businesses have to start differentiating themselves as others enter the market.

It is important to allocate resources toward promoting your business to your intended audience, but that doesn't just mean money.

If you are starting small, then your budget probably is too, and that's okay.

Your resources are not limited to money.

That's right, all promotion does not cost a lot of money. If you can spend some of your own time--your sweat equity--toward promoting your business you can focus on developing relationships and collaborations. If you are ambitious, create a networking group or an advertising co-operative if there isn't one you can join.

Another route to go is to bring in more talent to take on some of the tasks. Recruit a student public relations group or class to take you on as a client for the experience. Bring in an intern who can gain valuable experience to add to his/her résumé.

This isn't rocket science and does not need to be mind-boggling like many websites and books portray it. I have seen several businesses excel through good instincts and moxie. However, there is a science involved and Newton's laws of motion serve nicely as an analogy.

Apply these laws to small businesses, nonprofits, and even election campaigns. The principles are the same and have been simplified for a novice.

After reading this guide, you will have a firm understanding of the basics and will be ready to move forward promoting your business or nonprofit confidently. There are more sophisticated (and confusing) models out there, but you might never need those if you can master these principles.

Also included in this book is a fictional case study to help you see how the principles translate to practical implementation. When you are familiar with "The Laws of Promotion," you will be able to identify them in action with some of your favorite businesses and people in the public eye and with your newfound knowledge you will probably be able to identify what could be better for them.

Leslie A.M. Smith

Think about this …*One in five businesses fail in their first year of business.*

I believe that a contributing factor to a swift business closure (20% in their first year) is simply not promoting the business. Have you ever seen a restaurant or other business open near your home or where you work and it closed before you had a chance to go there? Maybe you even went there once or twice but were not surprised it closed. If yes, then picture that business and consider the following list to examine why they might have failed.

1. Had they coordinated any of the following?
    - Held a grand opening;
    - Distributed menus or coupons to the nearby neighborhoods;
    - Hung a banner or sign announcing their opening date;
    - Sent e-mails via your city's chamber of commerce or business district website;
    - Launched a social media presence promoting a "coming soon" message;
    - Earned a story in the local newspaper (print or online).
2. Do you know anyone who went there?
3. If so, was their reaction positive to create buzz about the opening?
4. Did the restaurant offer food that you and your neighbors or work colleagues like to eat?
5. Was the restaurant open when you're available to eat out?
6. Was it in an area you consider safe to visit?
7. Were the prices within your budget?

If the answers to some or all of these are also yes, then there was another factor that forced its closure. You might have heard why it closed in conversations with your friends and neighbors. Only some of these variables are in a business owner's control and changing them quickly can save the business.

1. Were expenses higher than budgeted (rent, food, or labor costs)?
2. Was the service bad or inconsistent?
3. Was parking a problem?
4. Did construction make it difficult to reach?
5. Was there a pandemic?

Building Blocks (Marketing Mix)

In starting any new product or service it is important to at least look at some basics of the marketing mix. These are known as the four Ps of the marketing mix: product, price, place, promotion.

Marketing is the umbrella term and should not be used interchangeably with its promotional elements, advertising and public relations.

Some models you can find on the Internet include more 'P's but I think many of the expanded list come later, mostly from strategy and are not at the most basic level. Stick with these and you'll do fine.

PRODUCT

Your product or service is what you are offering. The principle of supply and demand dictates that if you are supplying a product, demand for it is necessary to stay in business. "Demand" can be a want or a need, it really does not matter, but recognize which one you meet to predict the longevity of what you are offering.
- Is it seasonal, a fad, or eternal?
- Does it fill a universal need like toilet paper?
- Does it fill a seasonal need like umbrellas?
- Does it fill a location need like the requirement to use only clear purses at sporting and other large events?
- Does it solve a problem that no one has thought of before?

PRICE

The appropriate price is what the market will bear. There is a great deal of latitude between selling yourself short and gouging your customers. You don't want to do either, which means you need to do some research

If there is a lot of competition for your product or service, then you need to decide if your most unique attribute is a very high cost or a very low cost. For example, American Girl sells dolls for a little over $100 each. There are similar dolls called Our Generation sold at Target for $25-$40 each (regular to deluxe). One of these products is priced to be exclusive and one is readily available for the masses. Both sell for different reasons.

American Girl is selling an experience along with a very well-made doll. Each of their store locations include a restaurant, a hair salon, and even a doll doctor. American Girl is constantly expanding their clothing and accessories to go with the dolls, as well as children's sizes of the clothing to match. They also have companion books that fit the dolls in a historical perspective. In addition, they issue one special "Girl of the Year" doll for avid collectors.

Target sells their dolls and accessories amid hundreds of toys in hundreds of stores at a price most middle class people can afford. They are dolls with an assortment of extra outfits and some extra props. They do not include in-store experiences or extravagances—nothing exclusive.

PLACE

Where you offer your product can have a profound effect on how it is perceived and therefore purchased. Consider boutiques versus discount stores; home demonstrations versus catalogs; home-based versus office space; stand alone or in a mall, etc. Decide who your audience is and appeal to them where they are, both in-person and on the worldwide web.

When my daughters were young and interested in dolls, American Girl had stores in three cities—Los Angeles, Chicago, and New York. They now have closer to 20 stores, but to shop in their stores, and have the true American Girl experience remains pretty exclusive. These stores are strategically in cities where their clientele can afford and find value in taking a little girl to have her doll's hair done. As you can imagine, that won't work in every city.

Choose a location that allows your customers/clients/patients reach you easily.

PROMOTION

You have to promote your business!

Most simply, promotion can be divided into two main sections: advertising and public relations.

> **Advertising** is best thought of as "paid persuasion." Your message is delivered exactly how you want it, when you want it, where you want it. You dictate the size, the color, the placement, the look, when it runs, how often it runs, etc.
>
> **Public Relations (PR)** creates a favorable image through

behavior. PR is where you portray your core values: your dedication to the community through donations, your commitment to children through kid-friendly promotions, or your allegiance to your industry by playing a leadership role in a business organization.

Public relations can be further divided into several facets: press or media relations, community relations, public affairs, investor relations, just to name a few.

Both advertising and public relations are important. It can be affirming to see your favorite product advertised in your favorite magazine. It is even more powerful when you hear that your favorite product sponsors your favorite charitable cause. This creates strong brand loyalty. There are no guarantees with either of these promotional streams. You have to see what works best for you.

Where does social media fit? It seems to be the burning questions when I speak to small businesses and nonprofits. Social media is a tool of promotion, an outlet. There are many free options for social media and the many platforms provide conduits to express a consistent voice and branding. Social media includes opportunities for advertising and public relations. At this point, focus on your objectives and use social media only as it relates to those. Read this blog post for more details: https://www.mccormickla.com/tools-of-the-trade-social-media/

Through advertising and public relations you are aligning your company with your target market to ultimately reach long-term loyalty with your customers.

As we primarily address PROMOTION, you will notice that all four building blocks work together.

Sketch out your PRODUCT, PRICE, and PLACE for your product or service before you start your promotion. Know that they may change as you position your business effectively and grow it. Listen to your customers and constantly evaluate your success and failures.

Laws of Promotion

What are your marketing building blocks?
Here is a link to a downloadable version of this grid:
https://www.mccormickla.com/wp-content/uploads/2020/09/4Ps_2020_McCormickLA.pdf

Define them on a table like this:

Product	Place
Price	Promotion (Advertising & PR)

The First Law

Newton's First Law of Motion

A body remains at rest or in motion with a constant velocity unless an external force acts on the body.

Promotional Translation:
A business at rest stays at rest and a business in motion stays in motion unless someone or something interferes or intervenes.

Laws of Promotion

If you have not done anything to promote your business, you will stay at rest and could go out of business if you are not making enough money to cover all of your expenses and draw an income.

Putting things in motion creates momentum and activates outcomes.

Picture a lake. The lake represents your target market, or who will use your product. Right now you might not know exactly who. You might just know that they probably live in the same city or town as your business.

A business at rest looks out at a smooth, placid lake.

At rest it doesn't look like any fish are there.

A business in motion is busy with fish eating what the business puts out. You want to attract every fish you can in your lake.

Once you start promoting your business, the fish are jumping!

Hosting a grand opening or other event like a contest is like throwing fish food in the middle of that lake. You want to reach the entire lake and make all the fish take a bite.

Laws of Promotion

**You need to make sure of two things:
1) you are fishing in the right lake (PLACE), and
2) you are offering the right bait (PRODUCT).**

Build relationships with your customers and referral base.

A grand opening, or any event, has the potential of creating a wave of positive publicity, referrals and repeat customers. Activities at events are visually attractive to news cameras (print and broadcast) and can potentially draw a large crowd of would-be customers.

You stay in motion when you make it a priority to do so and it's always a priority!

People in business for themselves let their promotion activity stagnate when their workflow picks up. They secure a full client load, they work like mad for those clients, when the work is complete, they realize they have not been promoting themselves to potential clients. They have lost momentum and have to work harder to regain their pace.

The key is to have some proven mechanisms in place at all times. Advertising is a great way to keep feeding the lake while you are physically doing other things like client work and relationship building. Advertising is a physically passive form of promotion but it costs money. One-person businesses (solopreneurs) are spread thin. If your objective is to grow your business, then before you can afford to hire someone to help, advertising can help you secure sales/customers/clients.

Place ads in the lake where your fish swim or you will waste your money.

How To Coordinate a Grand Opening or Open House

Here's how you attract people to a grand opening. You will follow this same recipe for an anniversary celebration, product launch or other event, but a grand opening is your first opportunity to host an event.

Laws of Promotion

You send a press release to your local newspaper announcing your opening and what the mission of your business or nonprofit is to invite the public to your grand opening. Before you send that out, you've already planned the event with the assistance of your local chamber of commerce or business association. Because you submitted a nice story and were professional in your email, the local news will want to write a story about your upcoming event.

The story runs and draws customers to your event. It may generate another story about you and your new venture complete with an interview and photo. Interested people attend your grand opening and you collect their contact information as they enter a contest for a few prizes, including a free sample or consultation—whatever makes sense for what you sell.

Post photos and video of the event on social media as it happens. You supply a clever hashtag handle (#BestBizOpen—use your imagination!) and encourage people to post their own photos at the event. You might offer an incentive for them to do this.

After the event, send a thank you note to all the people whose info you now have, maybe include an incentive for them to come back. Depending on what kind of business you have will determine your next steps. Add them to a customer appreciation program or a monthly email. If you offer a service, follow-up with a call or send an email to make an appointment for a coffee or a lunch meeting. Ask them for their business and ask them for referrals.

This is how you build your network. You start developing satisfied customers who then tell their friends, who tell their friends, and so on, and so on … . You are now staying in motion as your momentum increases. Keep in touch with that reporter too. When you reach a milestone or choose to add a new product or service to your docket, you'll want a story about that too.

ACTIVITY: Self-Assessment

1. What are you currently doing that is moving your business or nonprofit in a forward direction?
   _____
   _____
   _____
   _____
   _____

2. Are there times you are staying at rest to your organization's detriment? If yes, what can you do to stop that?
   _____
   _____
   _____
   _____
   _____

CASE STUDY – PINT ONE
Brewser Beer

Brewser is a micro-brewing company that bubbled up from a home-brewed beer recipe. The developer, Brad, gave the beer to friends and family members as gifts for a few years before he decided to brew it for the general public's consumption.

Moving beyond a hobby, he started his business with the simple goal of selling a few six-packs and it being remembered as a great beer. His strategy with a very tight budget is to network and get his name out there. As a start-up business, he has a full-time job doing something else.

He knows that his target market is beer drinkers—specifically people who like craft beers. He knows that beer drinkers are mostly men but 30% are women. He found this information and many other beer drinking demographic facts just by searching on the Internet. He also paid attention to the feedback he received when he gave the beer to friends. The women he knows like Brewser beer, so he wants to make sure he includes them as a target market. This is especially important as most beer companies do not focus on women.

He plans to start promoting Brewser with these simple tactics:
• Attends weekly chamber of commerce meetings;
• Joins the local Brew Master Association and attends local meetings;

- Donates door prizes to the Women's Council and the Young Professionals business group;
- Joins a service club like Kiwanis or Rotary, attends weekly meetings and offers a discount on his beer for their mixers and holiday parties;
- Visits the local wine and spirits shops to encourage them to carry Brewser Beer;
- Sponsors local charity fundraisers with donations of gift baskets featuring Brewser Beer;
- Creates a website to promote the beer and launches social media pages;
- Begins merchandising with a few hats and t-shirts for family and friends.

Brad starts making some headway but he also is feeling some major strain on his personal life. He doesn't have time to do anything else.

Side Effects of Overdosing on Promotion:
A major hangover! This is too much for one person to do, especially as a side business. He needs to evaluate where he is benefiting and converting his relationships into sales. Once he knows that, he can focus on those activities, allowing the other things to fall away.

Laws of Promotion

ACTIVITY: Tactics

What simple tactics can you use to help you meet more people and make more sales? Make a list of five ideas right now and put a star next to the one you can do right away.

1. _____
2. _____
3. _____
4. _____
5. _____

The Second Law

Newton's Second Law of Motion

The force acting on an object is equal to the mass of that object times its acceleration.

$$F=ma$$

Simply put, the bigger something is, the more force or effort is needed to move it ahead.

It's easier to push a basketball than to push a car.

Laws of Promotion

Promotional Translation:

1. The *mass* of any organization (business or nonprofit) is measured by the number of employees, office square footage, geographic presence, revenue, clout, and its risks or liabilities.

2. The *acceleration* is determined by its objectives (the destination of the business: what and how much to accomplish, by when).

3. Multiplying mass times acceleration equals *force*, and force translates to the promotional activities required.

Leslie A.M. Smith

This chart helps you see how the mass determines how much force is required even when the acceleration is the same for a small or large business.

Second Law of Pro-Motion					
Mass		X	Acceleration	=	Force
Elements contributing to the mass of a business.	Small Mass Example	X	Objective	=	Promotional Tactics
Number of employees	2				- Local ads in a monthly neighborhood magazine. $ - Social media posts 3X/week (a few hours/week) $ - Promo discount. $ - Member of local business association. $
Number of locations	1		20% increase in sales over last year		
Office space	500 sq. ft.	X		=	
Goals/aspirations	Be #1 provider in your hometown				
Elements of business mass	Large Mass Example	X	Objective	=	Promotional Tactics
Number of employees	200				- Ads in nationwide publications and on a streaming service. $$$$ - Several social media platforms with posts several times every day. (One or more full-time employees)$$$$ - Presence at televised events. $$$$ - Sponsorship of an athlete. $$$$
Number of locations	3		20% increase in sales over last year		
Office space	25,000 sq. ft.				
Goals/aspirations	Be the #1 choice in the country	X		=	

Laws of Promotion

Remember that we learned with the First Law that if a business is at rest it will stay at rest unless acted upon. The Second Law tells us that not only will we need to keep the business moving forward, but to achieve certain goals or milestones (revenue, impact, products or services offered, etc.), within a specified timeframe, the force will need to be adjusted.

In terms of promotion, situations and opportunities are fairly equal regardless of mass. We'll label these opportunities our constants. Newton counted on gravity as a constant—it's the same everywhere, but for our purposes, a big company and a one-person shop can buy ads, send out press releases, curate a presence on social media, be active in the chamber of commerce or their respective business association, etc. Depending on how big the organization is, the force will be different.

Compare the largest company in your city or town to a small "mom and pop" shop. Depending on where you live and work, this comparison might be akin to comparing Disneyland to a school carnival. Think about the promotional activities (force) required for each of those to accelerate their businesses to show 20% growth in one year.

Because their mass is different, the force required is different to make an impact. Again, it takes more force to push a car than a basketball.

Larger companies need to invest in activities that make broader and deeper impact to move the needle toward the goal. Promotions may need to cover a larger geographic area as well.

Something to Think About – Forcing the Issue

This difference in "force" required is different for big and small companies in many ways beyond promotion. Think about how business leaders make decisions and steer their organizations. A one-person firm can make a decision quickly compared to how a large company typically makes decisions.

A smaller organization is nimble and can change fairly quickly. It's possible for both small and large companies to make swift decisions, but like a car, it is not as easy or as safe to flip a U-turn compared to changing a basketball's direction. I've witnessed larger companies that have someone at the helm who is empowered to make broad, sweeping, unilateral decisions. As much as that person might feel satisfied, the other executives and employees down to the rank and file are left with whiplash from sudden changes in direction, they may even take a hike.

As a business scales up, its leaders need to adjust their styles to do what the organization can handle and expect collateral damage when they choose not to adapt.

The bigger they are, the harder they fall.

Increased mass also includes increased clout, and a healthy side of risk. If a large organization has momentum but it is headed in a bad direction, it is like a car falling off a cliff. It will break apart, might even explode into a raging fire. Something with a smaller mass, like a basketball, might actually survive with a few hard bounces, or even avoid the fall. It could get pierced and deflated, but a patch kit is easy to find.

What are the results? Who else is hurt? There's more potential collateral damage from the car crash than the basketball.

A small business can change course quickly, rebound, and survive an occasional bad decision. Think about this in terms of a crisis situation.

If a three-person consultancy found out that their accountant was embezzling money from the company, the consultants can fire the person and file a lawsuit to get the money back. This is probably a private dispute and perhaps the long-term effect is that the consultants may have to work harder to make-up for any funds they could not recoup.

What if this happens to a large nonprofit and the money from several large donors has disappeared? Now several stakeholders, including the news media, are involved, hurt, and want to know what happened. The risk is much greater and affects many more people.

There is Safety in Numbers

Conversely, a small business can be more vulnerable. A single negative Yelp review is more detrimental to a small business with fewer customers compared to a bad critique of a large business that might serve several hundred customers a week and several positive reviews counteracting the one negative rating. It's important to know the risks.

CASE STUDY – PINT TWO
Brewser Beer

Goal: Brewser Beer is a leader in Southern California's craft beer market.

Objective: Increase sales by 20% with increased presence in two surrounding cities over the next two years.

His accelerant is geographic (place) and he's given himself two years. It's expanded from selling in his hometown of Long Beach, CA, and is modestly expanding into nearby cities. Southern California is densely populated. Expanding into two cities every two years can be an ongoing objective for geographic expansion to help him meet his goal while also growing his market share in Long Beach. How he does in the first two cities will help him decide whether and how to keep expanding.

His objective offers the parameters to accelerate this goal. It's relatively modest and realistic. Increase 20% in nearby cities. A 20% increase in sales over two years could be met if he replicates what has been working in Long Beach. Based on his research and familiarity in the area, he chooses San Pedro and Seal Beach.

If he wanted to increase the acceleration, he could increase the percentage or tighten the time frame. He is taking a conservative approach.

We multiply these two elements and we estimate how much promotion is required to make it all happen; to balance the equation.

Size X Objective = How much promotion we need
This is what our brew master decided needed to be done:

LOGISTICS:
- Production needs to increase so he sublet a brewing tank from a local brewery;
- Secure a supply chain (bottles/cans, labels, etc.) that will grow with Brewser's needs.

PROMOTION:
- Seek new outlets for Brewser in select cities (retail sales and restaurants);

Laws of Promotion

- Recruit salespeople in his two new cities (San Pedro and Seal Beach) to represent Brewser Beer at food and beer fests and other networking activities;
- Place social media advertising in the new areas, especially before events where Brewser will be served;
- Send a press release out to print and online sources in new markets;
- Join membership or business associations in San Pedro and Seal Beach;
- Create merchandising that extends his brand in the public's eye (cooler bags, reusable grocery bags, visors and ball caps).

As he strives to meet his objective, he might find he needs to increase his mass and hire a few more people to help coordinate events. With growth, his mass increases and the equation adjusts. More employees means more overhead and therefore more sales are needed to cover costs. Mass increases, acceleration increases, and the product of those two elements is increased force.

Brewser's Pro-Motion according to the Second Law				
Mass	X	Acceleration	=	Force
	X	Three accounts	=	Quarterly print ads Annual event Monthly tasting events Social media posts
Over the next two years …				
	X	15 Distribution accounts	=	Monthly ads Quarterly events Weekly tactics Social media posts, ads, and contests

Sir Isaac Newton would tell you that this is not real math. He's right, it isn't! You are applying common sense and intuition to estimate what you need. You know that a retailer like Amazon needs more force in its website than an independent jewelry store needs. You know that without any scientific calculation.

PRO-TIPS

1. *Phrase GOALS in present tense as if it is already true. Make them sound like affirmations.*

   Goal: Brewser Beer *is* a leader in Southern California's craft beer market.

2. *Start OBJECTIVES with active verbs.*
   Increase, Attract, Earn, Develop, Create, etc.

   Objective: <u>Increase</u> sales by 20% with increased presence in two surrounding cities over the next two years.

ACTIVITY: Objectives

Do you have business objectives written yet?
- You might have an income objective, sales territory or service area mapped out, and number of sales or clients you need to sustain your company or nonprofit.
- Writing these down helps give you direction and purpose. You are creating a map for your business success.

Write three business objectives:

1. _____
   _____
   _____
   _____

2. _____
   _____
   _____

3. _____
   _____
   _____

The Third Law

Newton's Third Law of Motion
For every action there is an equal and opposite reaction.

Action = Reaction
Seller = Purchaser
Ask = Answer
Give = Receive

Promotional Translation:
<u>Positive Actions</u>: In general, if you start your promotion there will be a reaction. People will support you or they won't.
That is the most basic concept.

<u>Negative Actions *Internally*</u>: If you cut corners in anyway, materially or ethically, there will be a reaction in the marketplace, quite possibly backlash.

<u>Negative Actions *Externally*</u>: If you do something negative to a competitor, there could be retaliation from the competitor or from your customers.

Let's look at this from the three points described above.
<u>First on the positive side</u>, when you first announce that your company or nonprofit exists and promote your call to action, some people will embrace it right away and react as you have asked and refer you more customers or clients. A portion of the people to whom you have communicated will identify themselves as not your market.

The biggest challenge is making sure you are fishing in the right lake,

Laws of Promotion

i.e. reaching your target market both for direct purchases/users and for referrals. You likely have some general idea of who your target market is when you started your business. "Who needs this?" is a fundamental question to ask before you spend any money or time on this endeavor. Figure out where those people are and what kind of bait they need to convert them into loyal customers and supporters.

When you are asking the right people, you are more likely to gain buyers.

You also probably have a circle of people who support you but are not in your target market. This level is mostly friends and family who support you no matter what and might be able to refer you clientele. These are all equal and opposite reactions; stimulus and response.

Offer = Buy or Refer

Maintain Balance

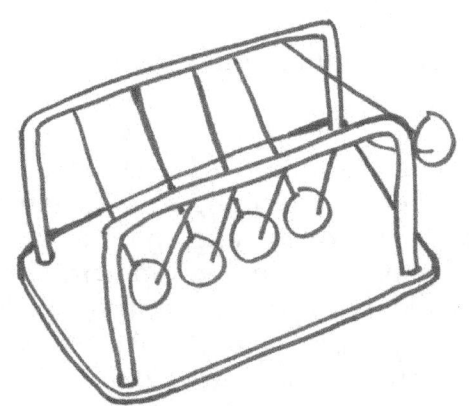

This is called a Newton's Balance Cradle, also a Balance Pendulum. Once that ball on the right drops (action), it will send its energy through the balls and make the ball on the very left bounce out as high as we can see the ball on the right is (reaction). This will continue almost perpetually, because a body in motion stays in motion unless acted upon (Newton's First Law). As one ball is pulled up and let go to swing the energy flows through and creates momentum.

Secondly, if a business goes <u>negative</u> it will be either an internal or external transgression. You've likely witnessed these tactics watching candidates wage against each other in a political campaign.

Internally: We've learned of stories in the past of companies knowing about the detrimental attributes of their products that they chose to keep quiet. Likewise, politicians' misbehavior in their personal and business lives are brought to light by their opposition trying to destroy their reputation. Once the whistle is blown and the tabloids have spoken, the equal and opposite reaction is demonstrated through sales or support diminishing (at least temporarily). Allegiance can return if the issue is explained and there's an apology. It is sometimes discovered that the claim was erroneous.

False Rumor = Truth, possibly coming out in a libel suit

Factual Deceit = Denial
Or
Factual Deceit = Punishment when found guilty by a jury or admission of guilt + a payout, public apology, or some other remedy

Externally: A tactic to explore if there is competition in your niche is to go head-to-head with a competitor.

Coke vs. Pepsi is a classic example. Both have similar colas that differ primarily in taste, and therefore in ingredients. Beginning in 1975, Pepsi set out to prove that the public preferred Pepsi over Coke. In blind taste tests that appeared in television commercials, a person would drink both colas without them being identified as Coke or Pepsi and choose which taste they preferred. More than 50% of the people chose Pepsi over Coke. Though Pepsi ran this campaign a number of times, Coke's reaction was not to launch another challenge of their own. I presume the risk would be they'd find the same thing.

Even though this is not a nasty battle, it evidently bothered Coke's executives enough that in 1985, Coca-Cola reacted to Pepsi's taste test results with a new recipe to change the Coca-Cola formula. It was disastrous! Funny thing is that Coke's sales outperform Pepsi's, then and

Laws of Promotion

now—Pepsi didn't gain new loyal customers. Also, it could be that taste alone is NOT why cola drinkers buy Coca-Cola over Pepsi.

There are many famous corporate battles: Microsoft vs. Apple (operating systems), Apple vs. Samsung (smartphone), Xbox vs PlayStation, and even DC vs Marvel Comics, to name a few. Most of these rivalries result in better products (and movies) for the consumer and we are spared from knowing what might be going on behind closed corporate doors.

Where we see plenty of public mudslinging is in politics. Politicians go head-to-head all the time to differentiate themselves from their opponents and they can become very controversial. These days it seems everything can be explored and exploited. There's backlash from the voters sometimes—the candidate does not always win the vote of an undecided voter because the voter may be disgusted by smear tactics.

There are times when a claim is made against a company or individual that is just plain hogwash. Many turn out to be urban legends or false accusations to benefit the person starting the rumor. The truth comes out so be honest and err on the side of protecting the public. You will not lose customers who feel you are looking out for their best interest.

When Johnson & Johnson faced the tragedy of someone poisoning bottles of Tylenol in stores, they found themselves recalling every single Tylenol product. They repackaged their product using tamper-proof methods and maintained respect and trust by sticking to their mission.

Leslie A.M. Smith

Case Study – Pint 3
Brewser Is Accused of Shorting Kegs

A local restaurant owner, Ronnie, who buys kegs of Brewser accuses Brad, Brewser's owner, of shorting the kegs. In a full keg, there is usually around 62 pints (16 oz. in a pint). Account for some spills here and there and you can bank on at least 58 pints. The disgruntled restaurateur, who also sells his own beer label, confronts Brad and Brad denies it.

Ronnie is not satisfied so he calls a local reporter who covers restaurants, food, and entertainment. The reporter is slightly interested and calls Brewser. Brad has already asked his other clients if they have noticed anything amiss with the keg quantity, no one has. When the reporter calls, Brad once again denies the accusation and takes advantage of this frivolous charge to pose a challenge for charity. Brad tells the reporter he will get back to him and calls Ron to respond by creating something positive, instead of a libel suit.

Ron loves Brad's idea and "Keg-Gate" is borne! For a $40 donation to the local Women's Business Incubator Foundation, beer drinkers gather one night to indulge in free-flowing beer and food to see how the kegs measure up. The men split the costs of the food and host it at the restaurant. They each donate five kegs for the event. All ten kegs are emptied, they added a drawing for gift cards and sold $2,000 in drawing tickets. They raise a total of $10,000 to donate to the charity. The results

Laws of Promotion

show that all kegs were within two ounces of each other. No trend for shrinkage for either label.

The reporter attended and drafted a great story.

Let's examine this against the Third Law of Motion. Action (a negative accusation), plus an equal and opposite reaction (a positive challenge for charity), galvanized into a collaborative event that helped both businesspeople and a charity.

What really happened?
At some point during the night one of the restaurant's servers explained to Brad that Ronnie gives employees a free pint of the house beer for every shift worked. Some of the servers prefer Brewser over the house label. So even though they enter the complimentary sale as the house beer, they pour themselves a Brewser. The same time the Brewser keg probably appeared short in the electronic inventory, the house kegs would have been overflowing.

Although it's tempting, Brewser does not launch a taste challenge of his own. The risk of such an action would be an equal and opposite reaction—jeopardizing his wholesale channels.

Evaluation

Like Newton, you need to behave like a good scientist and evaluate the outcomes of your promotional activities.

How do you know your promotional activity is working? Like the **First Law** says, when moving forward you will keep moving forward unless acted upon by an outside force. As it will seem like you are picking up momentum, how will you know for sure? Is it sales, visitors, more donors? Whatever is important to you should be the guideposts to measure your success. These items will be determined in your goals and objectives. Increase number of customers, sales, cost per sale, units per sale—whatever it is you have determined.

Have you been applying enough force as described in the **Second Law**? Unless you are the next best thing since sliced bread, you cannot only hang an open sign and expect people to find you and make you successful.

Finally, are you asking for business so your target market and referral sources can balance that action with an equal and opposite reaction as explained in the **Third Law**?

This form will help you see what call to action works for you with which media and help you determine what the most successful activities are for you. Your reasons for determining success will be different than for others. The form will also make you realize you have to ask people how they heard about you. You can use a pop-up form on your website, ask them at the point of service, or even as an exit question, but you must ask in order to discover which of your activities are working or not working.

Message Assessment Tool

Use the below chart to keep track of the many communications efforts you develop. You can download a chart from this blogpost: Visit https://www.mccormickla.com/evaluation-a-necessary-evil-that-i-make-easy/

Assess the promotional pieces that you might have in place:
- Collateral – letterhead, business cards, basic info brochure(s)
- Special event or fundraiser promotion – invitations, posters, accompanying ads
- Community events – free to attend (info symposium or informational fair)
- News media coverage – print, broadcast, online news sources
- Social media – Facebook, Twitter, Instagram, LinkedIn, blogs, etc.
- Advertising – service and event promotion.

Promotional Piece or Effort (e.g. letter, ad, brochure, phone calls, etc.)	Call to Action if any (Donate, join, attend, etc.)	Resources (staff, $, outside resources)	Results (# of Constituents reached, $ brought in, other tangible results)	Audience Reached (constituents, donors, referrals, board members, etc.)

Place a * next to your most successful pieces.   © McCormick L.A. Public Relations

Conclusion

My aim is to make marketing and promotions simple yet expose the rationale behind the methodology. It is not an exact science, but even at a very basic level, successful marketing includes a plan and a vision.

Your first steps are to plot out your Four Ps—product, price, place, promotion. If you are just now starting your business or nonprofit, or just now realizing you need to promote your business or nonprofit, be open to change. You might find out really quickly that your target market would be more willing to use you if you change something.

Once you start promoting your business, follow these simple laws, just like Isaac said.

1. Stay in Motion.
2. Adjust your promotional tactics (force) to accelerate your business or nonprofit to meet your objectives as your size changes.
3. For every action you take there is an equal and opposite reaction—Keep it positive!

Finally, evaluate what tactics are working and do more of those.

When the tactics don't work anymore or you are no longer moving forward, revisit your product, price and place. Things change and you can too.

Sign-up for my free e-newsletter by visiting my website at www.McCormickLA.com and if you enjoyed this guide, please leave a review on Amazon, it would be a great help to me.

Promotion Glossary

Advertising – Paid persuasion. You pay for the look, the content, and the placement of the ad. Also see Paid Media.

Digital Marketing – Any marketing that leverages virtual properties on the Internet.

Earned Media – When print, broadcast, and digital (includes blogs and other influencers) sources choose to write a story about you. You did not buy the coverage and you do not own the outlet.

Owned Media – This includes anything that you own and have complete control over. Your website, brochures, anything you have had printed, personalized SWAG, etc. Also called 'marketing collateral.'

Paid Media – If you paid for your ad or name to be there and you don't own it, it is paid media.

Promotional Assets – See owned media.

Public Relations – Creating interactions with people who can use your product or services, can refer you to people who need you, and can endorse what you offer. These activities largely build your community.

Social Media – Several online platforms that connect you to people who are connected to other people. It is also referred to as social media because the platforms largely exist without instructions and people will ask other people how it works and how to use it, creating more social interaction.

SWAG – An acronym for "something we all get." Any give away items you share with existing and prospective clients. Also known as "scientific wild ass guess" when someone gives a best guess at an answer based on some of the information.

Target Market – Your ideal client.

Pitch the Media – Leads to "earned media" what we used to call press or publicity.

ROI – Return On Investment. You gain something from investing your time, talent, or treasure (a monetary investment).

SEO – Search Engine Optimization. This is a technique to position your website in a way that Google, Bing, and other Internet search engines find you using your name and/or other keywords that categorize what you offer.

Acknowledgements

This guidebook started as a presentation in the 1990s delivered to small business groups. I always thought it had more potential and I am proud to finally put it in physical form.

The time to compile this was an unexpected gift of the 2020 COVID-19 pandemic as most of my business in community relations became impossible to administer.

Thank you to my family, Dennis, Blaire, and Jenna, for reading first drafts and taking care of the dinner dishes every night. My writing gals, Bonnie, Julie, and Olga, for encouraging me to finish any writing I start.

To the executives and staff members who run chambers of commerce and business associations across the country, cheers to you for being champions of small businesses, nonprofits, and solopreneurs in your community. You play a vital role in growing the economy.

A special thanks to Frank Buono, Kristine Hammond, Jeremy Harris, and Carolina Quezada for providing expert insights about businesses and nonprofits.

About the Author
Leslie A. M. Smith

Beginning her career at an Orange County advertising agency, Smith soon made a shift to association management and served as the communications director for local and statewide membership associations where she performed various public relations and community outreach functions.

Since founding McCormick L.A. Public Relations in 1994, she has developed and implemented marketing and public relations programs that include grand openings, product launches, social initiatives, and other community relations activities that earned her clients front page and network news coverage. She has worked with businesses of all sizes covering several industries: nonprofit organizations, aerospace, food services companies, business associations, real estate, restaurants, medical devices, professional services, departments of transportation, water districts, and so on.

To put it bluntly, she's done a lot! No matter what industry she was helping, she applied the same concepts every time for successful promotions.

She holds a Bachelor of Arts degree in Communications and a Minor in American Studies from California State University, Fullerton, and a professional writing certificate from California State University, Long Beach. She is a proud resident of Long Beach, California where she and her husband (and their rescue dog) raised their two daughters.

Visit her website: https://www.McCormickLA.com and sign-up for her e-newsletter for loads of promotional tips and creative insights.
Facebook: https://www.facebook.com/McCormickLA
Instagram & Twitter: @McCormickLA_PR

www.ingramcontent.com/pod-product-compliance
Lightning Source LLC
Chambersburg PA
CBHW070858220526
45466CB00005B/2037